I Know You!!

An Invitation from God

'Let's be friends!"

By

Michelle Green

The kind of intimacy and relationship we long for calls to us from our creator. He knows us better than we know ourselves, and he likes us!

I KNOW YOU!
An Invitation From God "Let's Be Friends!"

The kind of intimacy and relationship we long for calls to us from our creator. He knows us better than we know ourselves, and he likes us!

Testimonials

Michelle's book adequately titled comes from her own struggles and victories in her journey to understanding true intimacy with the Lord. Her simple and practical application portrayed in the book surprisingly challenged me to explore my own depth of intimacy with the Lord. "I Know You!" caused me to have an epiphany of God's profound love for me in spite of any shortcomings and His true desire to spend time with me and be my friend." - **Judy Bishop**

God knows me and wants to be my friend??? Such a simple concept. I never really felt that God knew me personally and never thought of a relationship with the Lord as a "friendship". Michelle Green's insightful, funny and down to earth "invitation" to become friends with God has changed that. She writes with a passion for her Lord in a way that is easy to understand and entertaining. Her words have left me eager to explore and develop that type of relationship with the Lord and I have accepted her "challenge" to go deeper and to truly experience a close and intimate friendship with my Creator. STOP LOOK & LISTEN... and you will find He is present in your life. I look forward to the answers I will get on this journey and thank Michelle for opening this door for me. - **Liz Q. Thomas**

"Michelle Green has a depth about her and she is a powerful and authentic woman of God. I believe this is because she knows God as her Lord and Savior and precious friend, but also truly has discovered the secrets to intimacy with Him. As David had, she has a heart after God's heart and knows Him as a true friend. I challenge you to get this treasure into your hands and watch as your relationship with Jesus will grow to depths you have not experienced before. Thank you Michelle for daring to risk in writing your book as it has personally blessed me. I am sure this is just the first of many treasures yet to come and it is my great pleasure to see you spread your wings in the fullness of your ministry and calling!" - **Claudia Santiago**

International Recording Artist, Speaker, Author, Actor, Coach – www.ClaudiaSantiago.com
CEO of www.VivaLaVidaSuccess.com and www.vpgroupinternational.com

Table of Contents

Introduction

I would like to invite you on a short journey with me. On this journey I will walk with you and introduce you to someone that longs to be your best friend. The desire in our heart to be known, understood, accepted, and loved unconditionally is possible when you meet your creator and he calls YOU friend. The journey between you and me is short; the friendship with the Lord is beyond a lifetime. Right now and exactly in your current details, the Lord longs to be your friend. Turn the pages and let's begin our journey into the greatest friendship you'll ever know!

Michelle Green

Chapter One

Cultivate Awareness

Let's Get Real

Insecurity in large groups caused me to miss out on a lot of wonderful relationship opportunities during my son's school age years. At the end of eight years in the same elementary and junior high school, I could not match most of the parents with their son or daughter. I simply had focused on the relationships developed in my comfort zone and wasn't aware of the rest. Not being aware of the other parents didn't make the parents non-existent. Many joys, triumphs, heart ache, laughter, and tears happened in the lives of many around me while I lived unaware. I was fully engaged in what I was fully engaged in but missed out on so much. I feel the effects of this when I run into someone and know they are a face from that era but cannot specifically ask them about their son or daughter.

I made many claims to fame with my ability to hyper focus on my husband at a restaurant, miss an entire building project taking place next to a stop sign

I frequent every day of the week, and didn't notice community landmarks, business, and building changes. If he was driving, I complained I had to watch the road because 'HE' was looking around! I did this, of course, with an air of righteousness. I was a safe driver and he needed to be; I was totally into our time together and wanted to give him my full attention. He could learn from that of course, his attention span with me needed work. Naturally, I could go on with more defenses on how wonderful I was – am. However, yes, there is a however. The truth be known, my ability to hyper focus which served well in many situations also deemed me many times, wait for it, clueless! Ugh! I eventually find out my claim to fame in relationships had wonderful qualities with room for improvement. I learned there was an entire world out there around me besides the tiny one I focused on, I discovered deeper relationships and events and places right in front of me I had never noticed. I had to cultivate awareness. No worries; In cultivating that awareness I figured out my husband could be observant at the same time giving me his attention, safely drive, and totally know what was going on in the community; so much for that air of righteousness.

Deuteronomy 31:8
The Lord himself goes before **you** *and will be with* **you;** *he will* **never leave you** *nor forsake* **you.** *Do not be afraid; do not be discouraged.*

Matthew 28:20
I am **with you** *always, to the very end of age.*

And so it is with God, whether we are aware of it or not God is with us, always. He tells us this and he never leaves us. In the same way I had to purpose to become aware of my surroundings and life outside my norm, we have to choose the journey towards an awareness of God.

Matthew 7:7-12
[Ask, Seek, Knock] Ask and it will be given to you; seek and you will find; knock and the door will be opened to you. For everyone who asks receives; the one who seeks finds; and to the one who knocks, the door will be opened.

Let's start this journey by taking a second or even a minute and choose to look around and know he is in your present.

I had to make a conscience effort to look around at my surroundings when I was in public or private; I had to ask questions when I was with acquaintances about their lives and invest the time to actually listen and hear. This didn't come naturally to me and it is still something I have to make a conscience effort to do. Yet, I am better than I use to be and the journey has been rewarding. I am still learning to cultivate this awareness and it has been liberating to learn God is in the ordinary and mundane details of our everyday lives.

What are we looking for in that moment we choose to take notice? Well, do it now. **Stop reading for 15 seconds and look around.** What did you see? What did you hear? He is in the laughter, the tears, the rain, the sunshine, the sweet babies, the flowers, the snow, the animals, your heartaches, and your triumphs. He is there. He is longing and calling out to you to be noticed by you. That's right his heart hurts to know you better; his heart longs to be noticed in your everyday details. He loves you perfectly and completely and wants to meet you in the depths of your heart and awareness; he wants what we long for, relationship.

Challenge:
Whether you are just beginning this journey or been on it for a while, over the next SEVEN (minutes, hours, days, or weeks) purpose to stop SEVEN

(times an hour, day, or week) and begin or deepen your awareness of God's presence in your present.

Practical Application:
Stop! Look! Listen! What do you see? What do you hear? Spend time becoming aware of His presence wherever you are and whatever you are doing. Get creative and alert yourself in some way every day to make a conscience decision to cultivate an awareness of God's presence in your present. Perhaps use one of the following suggestions:

- Set an alarm on your phone several times a day to stop, look, and take a moment. Ask a question or mention, "I know you are here" or "Are you here?"
- Place sticky notes in different locations you pass frequently throughout the day to prompt you to stop, look, listen, ask questions, or simply take notice.
- Perhaps jot down different times you were aware; something you heard or something you saw or thought.

Now that you have decided to begin or deepen your awareness of God in your everyday details, and after you have spent some time practicing and creating the habit to cultivate that awareness, when you are ready turn the page and we'll talk more about God's real and tangible presence.

Let's Pray:
Heavenly Father,
You long to make us aware of you as you are certainly aware of us. As we begin this journey of cultivating an awareness of you, Lord, be with us. Open our eyes to see and our ears to hear; make us sensitive to your presence in our present. Lord, put a hedge of protection around each of us as we open our hearts to you.

We praise you and thank you in your son's name, Jesus. Amen

Chapter Two

Engage Presence

First Impressions

Sometime over our lifetime I am certain all of us have first impressions that we've later discovered were wrong. Three occasions come to mind easily for me and all three ended with surprisingly different outcomes than I would have expected. Two of the occasions were work situations left to first impressions would have been a tragic loss of what turned out to be wonderful friendships. The third was a more significant challenge and took a decision to respond different than the original reactions to the other person involved. My first impression on how I was being treated was not only an impression but a truth witnessed by others. It took longer than I care to admit but I finally took the relationship to the Lord in prayer and that decision turned into a reluctant journey of turning things around. In God's infinite wisdom he lead me to discover the actions of the other person turned out to be filtered through years of hurt and insecurity and for some reason I had become the object of her release. Had God simply granted my request for her to stop or to tell me what the deal was instead of commanding me to befriend her, the eventual friendship that lead to ministry time, healing, and my complete release of offense would have never happened. God had a plan that I did not.

All of our relationships start where we started in the last chapter becoming aware. Whether we first become aware of someone because of work environments, social settings, or by hearsay, it's after that we choose to interact or choose not to. It would have been much easier to skip the initial effort it took to move past my first impressions but had I made that choice I would have missed out on these relationships that have in some way significantly influenced my life.

Over the years I've heard different ones express they believe in God but he is more like a distant cousin or some far away concept or idea instead of someone they can really relate too. In fact, it wasn't until my adult life that I came to really understand the possibility of having a real and interactive relationship with God. How about you? Does the idea seem a little far-fetched? Let me tell you when

I Know You

I first met these three people I would have bet money we wouldn't become friends; frankly, I didn't really have a desire to even contemplate the idea. Being aware of God and choosing to engage in His presence is something you'll someday wonder how you survived without.

In the last few days, you've stopped and looked seven different times during your day to cultivate an awareness that God was in your midst (in your daily details). Let's take it to the next level. This week stop, look, and what? Stop, look, and listen? Stop, look, and say something. This week when you take the moment or 60 seconds to stop and become aware of God in your details choose to interact with Him. You can see someone every day in the break room at work or the counter at a quick mart or any place you frequent daily. You are certainly aware of them; however, unless you choose to interact with them you are simply aware of their presence nothing more. Perhaps you choose to interact at first by stopping long enough to notice something about that person instead of an absent minded acknowledgment. You start to notice qualities or similar interest and eventually choose to stop and genuinely comment or ask a question. Stop, look, and say something. What? How about, "I know you are here." Or, "Are you really here?" Or, "Thank you for being here." Or, whatever comes to your mind. Or stop, look, and listen. What do you hear in your heart? Sometime during the day jot down what you said or heard. You may be aware several times during the day and only speak or listen once or twice. It is your journey. The key is to begin and to choose not to skip the initial effort.

You can never establish a personal relationship without opening up your own heart. ~Paul Tournier

Challenge:
Continue your journey on cultivating an awareness of God in your daily details. Begin to engage in His Presence in your present.

Practical Application:
Stop! Look! Listen! Stop. Look. Speak. Over the next few days as you become aware of God's presence choose to engage by speaking or asking a question. "Thank you for being here." "I know you are here." "Are you REALLY here?" You decide what you would like to say in that moment. Make this journey yours as you creatively choose different ways to engage God's presence in your present. Perhaps use one of the following suggestions:

- Pick a number and associate it with becoming aware; when you see that number stop a moment and ponder, speak, listen, or simply look around and notice. Interact by commenting or asking a question.
- Set an alarm on your phone several times a day and stop, look, and take a moment. Ask a question or mention, "I know you are here" or "Are you here?"
- Place sticky notes in different locations you pass frequently throughout the day to prompt you to stop, look, listen, ask questions, or simply take notice.
- Perhaps jot down different times you were aware in something you heard or something you saw or thought.

You have begun the journey of cultivating an awareness of God. This week you are going to practice engaging in his presence. When you are ready turn the page and we'll discuss [what difference does it make anyway] to know He exists or interact with His existence.

Let's Pray:
Thank you for being with us, Lord. This week take us to the next level. Show us how to engage in your presence. Prompt us to ask questions or make

comments. Help us know you more and recognize you in our details. Thank you, Lord, for wanting to journey with us as we come to know you in our everyday lives.

We thank you and praise you in the Name of Jesus, Amen.

Chapter Three

Acknowledge Existence

Why Bother? Cultivate. Engage. Acknowledge.

Why bother to cultivate awareness, engage in the presence, or even acknowledge the existence?

For as long as I can remember I've always liked to entertain. For many years I loved all the hoopla of coordinating food and decorations around themes, surprises, and whatever I could do to add flavor and an element of wow to the occasion. There is something about creating atmosphere and ambience motivated out of love that makes others feel special. I enjoyed bringing joy to others through this expression. Until I outgrew this expression it was a labor of love, easy, and fun. Eventually, years turned into a few decades and the labor of love became labor. What was once easy and fun became busy, expensive, and time consuming. I simply had outgrown this season in my life. I didn't transition from hoopla to my current entertainment disposition easily. Currently, social gatherings at my house are no longer theme based, coordinated, and time consuming; in fact, they are not even about the menu. Rewind several years back and it would be unbelievable I would ever be able to state this current fact. After the hoopla era it was just work. I wanted to have family and friends over; I just didn't know how not to make a fuss. Hoopla turned into worrisome cooking and cleaning and no time to visit. By the time dinner was cooked and the dishes cleaned, everyone else was all tuckered out and ready to go home. Finally, the cultivating awareness days sparked an epiphany. I didn't fully know what was going on in the lives of those closest to me; I depended on my husband to tell me what I missed while I was being busy. I was not engaged in those around me; I was not present in their presence. Although journeying through awareness has been wonderful it certainly hasn't been without regret. However, I only allow myself small doses of grief; I've wasted enough time not realizing the limits of my small world. Now social events at my house consist of whatever food sounds good and easy at the time; no one wash dishes or worries with clean up. If everything is ready when the guest/family/friends arrive, fine, if not, we finish up together. I simply sit. I talk. I listen. I laugh. I cry. I engage in the presence of those around me in my present. My relationships are astonishingly more enriching and satisfying. Opening up to those around me and expanding my world enriched my life when I didn't know it needed enriched and continues.

We might know God exist and acknowledge His existence. We might have a strong belief and reverence for His existence. This knowledge and belief are hope for eternal salvation. It brings comfort. The original question was why bother. Why bother to become keenly aware of His presence in your everyday details and engage in that presence? To be fully engaged in His presence opens the doors to a real and tangible relationship that can bring more and complete satisfaction than any relationship you've ever experienced to-date. It is worth the bother to choose the journey to friendship; it's a journey worth taking. Your life will be truly enriched.

Recently, someone said to me, "I've not forgotten you; I have big plans for you." That statement brought me hope and a peace that I was on the right track as far as this particular person and community go. However, right now my relationship with this person is based on what I know about her and my involvement in a community she is involved in with only occasional personal contact. I am excited about this relationship; it is the beginning of a relationship I am certain will lead to a lifetime friendship. Our relationship with the Lord takes a similar journey. Our choice to become keenly aware and choose to spend time with the Lord will lead us to knowing him and his plans; and ultimately will lead to an eternal friendship. He knows us; he wants us to know Him He longs for this union.

Jeremiah 1:5
Before *I formed* **you** *in the womb I knew* **you, before you were born** *I set* **you** *apart; I appointed* **you** *as a prophet to the nations.*

Jeremiah 29:11
For I know the **plans** *I have for* **you,"** *declares the Lord,* *"***plans to prosper you** *and not* **to** *harm* **you, plans to** *give* **you** *hope and a future.*

Challenge:
Make a decision to really apply these relationship building blocks to build a strong foundation. Practice and then practice some more! Make your awareness and engaging in God's presence real. Ask questions. Listen. Jot down thoughts about how you feel, what you think, what you notice and anything else that will help you recognize changes throughout your journey. Create a habit of seeking him. Determine to do this. Do this in your everyday details; make Him a part of your life right now where you are.

Practical Application:
Stop. Look. Listen! Stop. Look. Speak.
• Read, ponder, or memorize the meanings of the scriptures we have mentioned so far. Find scriptures that speak to you and jot them down and read them over and over.

- Pick a number and associate it with becoming aware; when you see that number stop a moment and ponder, speak, listen, or simply look around and notice. Interact by commenting or asking a question.
- Set an alarm on your phone several times a day and stop, look, and take a moment. Ask a question or mention, "I know you are here" or "Are you here?"
- Place sticky notes in different locations you pass frequently throughout the day to prompt you to stop, look, listen, ask questions, or simply take notice.
- Perhaps jot down different times you were aware in something you heard or something you saw or thought.

You have become aware of God's presence. You have decided and practiced engaging in His presence. You've determined His existence in your daily details is going to be worth the effort to notice. After you feel deeply connected to this strong foundation, you'll turn the pages four more times to explorer intimate friendship finding it adds to your life favor, power, and authority.

Let's Pray:
Lord,
Thank you for the last few days as you have shown yourself to us and continue to do so daily. We

praise you. Call to our minds thoughts of you. Let us hear the knock on our hearts and respond with a yes. Help us to firmly build the foundation on our hearts to receive your invitation to intimate friendship. Show us how to journey with you to fulfill your heart's desire for our lives. We say yes. In the name of Jesus we pray. Amen

Chapter Four

Friendship

Longing for More

The evening was beautiful outside. In fact, it was probably nearly perfect with the temperature, sun shining, the breeze, and the company I was keeping (my husband). We walked in silence most of the time but the connection was there. It was all very simple. It was nice. It was peaceful and fulfilling. I started thinking about the effort I had put into writing something for this friendship chapter. Suddenly I felt like the Lord gently impressed on my heart, "I like this too; just being together on this quiet walk." The impression went on to suggest that friendships at their best are comfortable in the silence. It was like I could hear God saying, "I enjoy what you enjoy. I am with you always; I'm in your thoughts, in your heart, in your conversations. I am in your day to day details. Recognize me in all things and choose to interact with me. Two-way friendships are the best. I want to share my heart with you and my desires as much as I want you to share yours with me." Wow, could it be that simple? In our human experience relationships have a tendency to be more complicated. We filter them through life circumstances, good and bad experiences, perceptions, and a ton of other influences all wrapped up in the confinement of time and physical location. It's exciting to realize friendship with God is not constrained by time and geographical locations because He transcends both.

Set aside the fact that writing this chapter was difficult because there is nothing new to report. There are more books, movies, greeting cards, tweets, posts, how to – when to suggestions, out there about friendships and relationships, what could I possibly add but another feel good story or my perception of what a friend should or shouldn't be; and that's just it, it would be my opinion based on me. It was difficult too because I still see myself barely out of the starting gate in learning to be two-way friends with God. During one my many sessions of writing, adding and deleting, I finally wrote I was not enjoying what I was writing. Lord, I typed, if I am bored and not engaged in what I am writing, how can I expect anyone else to be engaged? I then asked Him what He would say to you or me about being friends with us. The following is a condensed version of what I felt like He was saying to you and me.

I know you. I get you. I created you. I know you better than you know yourself. If you knew you like I know you, you would smile and be pretty impressed with yourself. I mean impressed for real reasons not the ones you make up. The ones you are impressed with are from the gifts I give you so it doesn't call for you to be all that impressed. (*Chuckling Here*) I see what you don't see in yourself. It has absolutely nothing to do with what you do. It has to do with who you are.

Psalm 139:13-14 NIV
For you created my inmost being; you knit me together in my mother's womb. I praise you because I am fearfully and wonderfully made; your works are wonderful, I know that full well.

It has nothing to do with what you say or think. I know your thoughts and opinions are based on filters that are usually skewed. I know the real you. I like the real you. It isn't about what you deserve or do not deserve; it is about you. The real you hidden behind what you do, think, and say; you are not your good choices or your bad choices.

Hebrews 4:13
Nothing in all creation is hidden from God's sight. Everything is uncovered and lay bare before the eyes of him to whom we must give account.

I know you and I like you. So much so I long to spend time with you.

1 Corinthians 1:9
*God is faithful, who has **called you into fellowship** with his Son, Jesus Christ our Lord.*

What do you know about me? You know what you've heard. I want to share the real me with you. I want to be your friend. You are human and you have relationships based on the human experience. I want you to know you are made in our image; therefore there is a longing inside of you for more. I am that more. Even the most gifted philosophers and scholars, priests, ministers, theologians who know about me and experience me to some degree long for more. The human experience of cultivating a friendship definitely can apply to becoming my friend when you are first starting this journey. Take this journey seriously and I will fulfill the longing you have for more. Continue to develop the ability to sense my presence through awareness and the choice to engage. When you have purposed in your heart that it is worth the decision, what starts with effort I will make effortless. My friendship is a gift.

Isaiah 30:18
*Yet **the Lord longs to be gracious to you**; therefore he will rise up to show you compassion. For the Lord is a God of justice. Blessed are all who wait for him!*

Jeremiah 29:13
*You **will** seek **me** and **find me** when **you** seek **me** with all **your** heart.*

We are a society that likes to give gifts. If someone gives you a gift you have a choice to receive the gift or to reject the gift. Once you take the gift you can then put it aside and forget about it and its value only lasted a moment. This journey is about receiving the gift of friendship the Lord offers us, staying aware and engaged, and keeping it close in our present.

Challenge:
Proverbs 3:5-6
*Trust **in the Lord with all your heart** and lean not on **your** own understanding; in **all your** ways submit to him, and he will make **your** paths straight.*

We are changing practical application to experience Him because we've spent time practicing and testing the waters and finally decided we want to be friends. Now it is time to experience more.

Experience Him:
- Stop right now and ponder some of the different ways you pursue friendships. In the same way pursue the Lord. The wonderful difference is He is always with you without the boundaries of time and location.
- Start engaging Him in conversation in whatever you have going on. Remember conversation is generally two ways, so listen in your heart for a response.
- Ask him questions and expect Him to answer. Having Him continually near is a wonderful way to get a different perspective at any given moment you are willing to Stop. Look. Listen.
- Continue engaging Him in the ways you've been practicing, setting your reminders and jotting things down.
- Don't forget this is your friendship; make it personal!

Spend some time experiencing Him on a daily and eventually a continual basis. When you are ready to turn the pages, we'll continue our journey together and redefine the phrase, 'friends with benefits' 'it is all in who you know'.

Let's Pray:
2 Corinthians 13:14
*May the grace of the Lord Jesus Christ, and the love of God, and the **fellowship** of the Holy Spirit be with you all.*

In Jesus precious name,
Amen.

Michelle Green

Chapter Five

Favor

Benefits Redefined

Friends with benefits is an expression I was hoping to search on the internet for a meaning other than the one I know it to be, simply casual sexual relations without commitment. It didn't take but a half a minute to discover it wasn't a phrase with some other meaning taken out of context. It actually came about in the mid 1990's meaning exactly what we've all known it to mean. Discovering that fact made me take pause and ask Holy Spirit if I had to shuck the idea of using it in this chapter. Nope. I'm going to use it. In this world it is popular to take something beautiful in meaning and turn it to something perverted, so why not take something meant for less than God's best for us and turn it around to mean something wonderful?

We have a swimming pool. One of my long time good friends has a schedule that allows her to swim during the day while we are working. Even though we are away, our relationship gives her the freedom to utilize our pool and home. That is a benefit of our friendship. On occasion she has asked to have someone I didn't know accompany her to swim. After a brief hesitation I gave my blessing. The first time we easily communicated our expectations of each other in this new scenario in our relationship. She didn't want to take advantage of me and I needed her to know my security laid in my trust in her and her judgment not the person she invited. The person my friend invited had my favor indirectly.

Hear me on this serious proclamation – Intimate friendship with the Lord is NOT a means to an end. We wouldn't call a friendship genuine if it were one sided or we were sought only when it benefited the other person. It would be dissatisfying at best. We are made in His image; therefore, the desires of our heart do not entirely differ from the desire of His heart. The difference usually lies in our perception of what would fulfill those desires. If I thought my friend only wanted to be friends because of what I may be able to provide for her, I wouldn't have categorized her 'one of my long time good friends'. Because she is a long time good friend, I first offered her the use of my pool and home at her leisure. The favor we receive from the Lord's friendship is so generous our generosity pales in comparison. In fact, I'll add that His generosity is so amazing in comparison all of our relationships look suspect.

The cool thing about being friends with the Lord as mentioned before, He is always with us. He knows everything about you and loves for you to talk to him about it. If we are trying to explain ourselves, it is merely an exercise for our own understanding because He actually knows us better than we know ourselves. He gets you! He delights in you. He sees your sorrows and your joys. He desires for you to know Him as intimately as He knows you.

Psalm 94:11
The Lord knows the thoughts of man; that they are a mere breath.

So what are some of these things we call having favor of the Lord?

Zephaniah 3:17
For the LORD your God is living among you. He is a mighty savior. He will take delight in you with gladness. With his love, he will calm all your fears. He will rejoice over you with joyful songs.

The thing is; even though friendship with the Lord is not a means to an end everything ends up well when he's involved. He wants to lavish His favor on us. All we have to do is ask! Would you dare ask an acquaintance for a favor with the same confidence you would ask a close friend? Our motivation to pursue intimate friendship with the Lord may begin with the payoff in mind, but like our current close relationships it is out of that intimacy we give and receive favor. Graham Cooke talks about the Holy Spirit being awesome company! He talks about the Holy Spirit being funny and how much it helps that the Holy Spirit is all knowing. The first time I thought the Lord humorously answered a flippant question I mindlessly asked him, I stopped in my tracks and exclaimed, "Did you just say what I thought you said!?" I don't know if I was more shock at the invasion of interaction or the answer. Why would I even think of it as an invasion of my thoughts? I had addressed the question to him. He really is there and He really talks. My journey is still in a place I enter in and out of awareness of His presence. I have journeyed long enough I guess it is fun for Him to remind me He is there – not just in concept or like you've probably heard me say if you've been around me very long, I have to stop talking to Him as though I were narrating a letter, text message, or leaving a voice mail. I wouldn't do that to my other friends in the same room with me.

Matthew 7:11
If you, then, though you are evil, know how to give good gifts to your children, how much more will your Father in heaven give good gifts to those who ask him!

John 21:20
Peter, turning around, *saw the disciple whom Jesus loved following them; the one who also had leaned back on His bosom at the supper... (This scripture added to show the comfort level between friends.)

Galatians 5:22-23
But the fruit of the Spirit is love, joy, peace, patience, kindness, goodness, faithfulness, gentleness, self-control; against such things there is no law.

Challenge:
Learn more about who God is and what type of favor is given from intimacy with him. Be intentional in getting to know God! Be aware He is in your present. Stop. Look. Listen. Speak.

Experience Him:
- Ask Him for the favor of peace if you are anxious about something. Expect Him to answer you.

- Do you need direction for a decision, ask for the favor of His wisdom; listen for His perspective.
- In my experience some situations He points out the positives in both and asks what you think; in others He presses a peaceful yes or an adamant cautious feeling. He is gracious and is a gentleman; He will not force you to do anything or to listen. He will, however, speak in His still small voice.
- Do a bible word search on one of His characteristics like comforter.
- Pick up a Promises of God book and let Him show you favor through making a scripture your own to stand on and talk to Him about.
- Ask Him to reveal His favor to you personally and touch your heart with new understanding in what it means to acknowledge Him and engage in relationship with Him.

Pick something and do it. Just do it.

Jeremiah 33:3
Call to Me and I will answer you, and I will tell you great and mighty things, which you do not know.
Proverbs 3:5-12
*Trust God from the bottom of your **heart**; don't try to figure out everything on your own. Listen for God's **voice** in everything you do, everywhere you go; he's the*

one who will keep you on track. Don't assume that you know it all. Run to God! Run from evil! Your body will glow with health; your very bones will vibrate with life! Honor God with everything you own; give him the first and the best. Your barns will burst your wine vats will brim over. But don't, dear friend, resent God's discipline; don't sulk under **his** loving correction. It's the child he loves that God corrects; a father's delight is behind all this.

Let's Pray: Help each of us, Lord, on our journey to know you as a friend. Let our friendship bless you too. Guide us on how to pursue you, recognize you, speak and listen to you. You are a friend with benefits; we thank you for your patience as we learn not to use you as a means to an end but instead to know you as intimately as you know us. You want to graciously show us what it means to have favor of the Lord; let us recognize and acknowledge it with praise on our lips and joy in our hearts!
In Jesus Mighty Name,
Amen

Michelle Green

Chapter Six

Power

Intimacy the Source

By now you've heard me speak of the nature of God and the fruits of His spirit; perhaps, not in those exact words but truly in your pursuit of friendship with the Lord you are discovering His nature and the different types of favor that flows from that relationship (the fruits).

Galatians 5:22
The fruit of the Spirit is love, joy, peace, forbearance, kindness, goodness, faithfulness, gentleness, and self-control.

(I looked up a synonym for forbearance in the dictionary and the word endurance came up along with many others.)

I mentioned before that Graham Cooke has been known to say hanging out with the Holy Spirit was outrageously fun; He is great company. Have you ever noticed after spending time having fun and connecting easily with a close friend you feel energized, peaceful, joyful? Great company has that effect on us. The simple choice to have an intimate friendship with the Lord causes the same effect plus more. He *is* love. He *is* joy, peace, endurance, kindness, goodness, faithfulness, gentleness, and self-control. There is a saying, Show Me Your Friends and I'll Tell You Who You Are. According to a blog on the internet one opinion is the saying typically is used with a negative and I found the bloggers entry insightful. However, I was only using the saying in fun gist to say how cool if I am hanging out with Holy Spirit you see His joy, peace, endurance, kindness, goodness, faithfulness, gentleness, and self-control reflected in my life! My husband played a great round of golf a while back and road that energy from the fun and fellowship with his buddies for at least a week. I enjoyed the fruits of that intimate time spent with his friends on the golf course. He was a pleasure to be around; his perspectives and responses were positive and easy. The same situations causing a need for a perspective or response on the heels of a rough people interaction work week leaving him dismayed and tired could have been completely different. Clearly, in the example of my husband after a great day with friends compared to a frustrating week at work we find the source of power behind our perceptions and responses can be somewhat influenced by the company we keep. Even at the most simplistic level of this discussion, keeping company with the Holy Spirit potentially can cause you to have His peace. That peace reflected in you can potentially affect those around you. Terry had a great day at the golf course with his friends causing peace and joy; I wasn't a part of that fellowship but I experienced the power resulting from his day. With much greater cause and effect, hanging out with Holy Spirit on a daily basis especially practicing the two-way part of friendship not only will fulfill you but will have the power to influence those around you by the reflection of His fruits in your responses to situations and your insight from Holy Spirit's perspective.

As you journey in this friendship with the Lord you will naturally progress through more discoveries of God's power and the power you have because of your intimacy with the Lord.

You will experience the power of the blood of Jesus.

Ephesians 2:13
*But now you have been united with Christ **Jesus**. Once you were far away from God, but now you have been*

brought near to him (fellowship) through the **blood of**
Christ *(parenthesis added by author)*
You will experience the power in the name of Jesus.

Philippians 2:10
So when the name of Jesus is spoken, everyone in heaven
and on earth and under the earth will bow down before
Him.

You will experience the power of endurance and
much more.

Psalm 28:7
The Lord is my strength and my shield; My heart trusts
in Him, and I am helped; Therefore my heart exults, And
with my song I shall thank Him.

Philippians 4:13
I can do all things through Him who strengthens me.

Psalm 62:7-8 (NIV)
My salvation and my honor depend on God;
he is my mighty rock, my refuge.

Psalm 62:7-8 (MSG)
My help and glory are in God
— granite-strength and safe-harbor-God —
So trust him absolutely, people;
lay your lives on the line for him.
God is a safe place to be.

Challenge:
Choose to stay close and aware of your friendship with the Lord and experience the bi-product of intimacy with him which is the fruits of the spirit. The power you personally experience in the different fruits has the power to affect those around you.

Experience Him:
- Continue to Stop! Look! Listen! Speak! Engage the Lord in your present!
- Go deeper and speak out loud some of God's promises over your life. I read there are too many promises documented in the bible to count; some have said well over 3,000. Have a conversation with the Lord and ASK Him which promise he would like to bring alive to you right now!
- Discover the power of the name of Jesus; if there are times you don't know what to say and time is limited say His name, this is acknowledging Him and expect just calling on the name of Jesus to have power to influence your moment. Keep Him close and present in your present.
- Laugh out loud with the Lord. If you listen he will say something in your heart and mind that is funny.

- Take notice that **He enjoys you. Have fun! The Message reads Ecclesiastes 5:19 to say-** Make the Most of What God Gives-After looking at the way things are on this earth, here's what I've decided is the best way to live: Take care of yourself, have a good time, and make the most of whatever job you have for as long as God gives you life. And that's about it. That's the human lot. Yes, we should make the most of what God gives, both the bounty and the capacity to enjoy it, accepting what's given and delighting in the work. It's God's gift! **God deals out joy in the present, the now.** It's useless to brood over how long we might live.

Friends with benefits take on a new meaning when referenced with our relationship with the Lord; The first benefit introduced was favor, now power, and when you are ready to move on to the next few and final pages, authority.

Let's Pray:
 Psalm 103 The Message (MSG)
1-2 O my soul, bless GOD.
From head to toe, I'll bless his holy name!
O my soul, bless GOD,
don't forget a single blessing!
3-5 He forgives your sins — everyone.
He heals your diseases — everyone.

I Know You

He redeems you from hell—saves your life!
He crowns you with love and mercy—a paradise
crown.
He wraps you in goodness—beauty eternal.
He renews your youth—you're always young in his
presence.
6-18 GOD makes everything come out right;
he puts victims back on their feet.
He showed Moses how he went about his work,
opened up his plans to all Israel.
GOD is sheer mercy and grace;
not easily angered, he's rich in love.
He doesn't endlessly nag and scold,
nor hold grudges forever.
He doesn't treat us as our sins deserve,
nor pay us back in full for our wrongs.
As high as heaven is over the earth,
so strong is his love to those who fear him.
And as far as sunrise is from sunset,
he has separated us from our sins.
As parents feel for their children,
GOD feels for those who fear him.
He knows us inside and out,
keeps in mind that we're made of mud.
Men and women don't live very long;
like wildflowers they spring up and blossom,
But a storm snuffs them out just as quickly,
leaving nothing to show they were here.
GOD's love, though, is ever and always,
eternally present to all who fear him,

Making everything right for them and their children
as they follow his Covenant ways
and remember to do whatever he said.
¹⁹⁻²² GOD has set his throne in heaven;
he rules over us all. He's the King!
So bless GOD, you angels, ready and able to fly at his bidding, quick to hear and do what he says. Bless GOD, all you armies of angels, alert to respond to whatever he wills. Bless GOD, all creatures, wherever you are—everything and everyone made by GOD.
And you, O my soul, bless GOD!
AMEN!

Chapter Seven

Authority

His

If you are practicing being aware of God's presence and engaging Him in your details; if you are journeying towards intimate friendship and experiencing the fruits of His Spirit with lavished favor and power, what need is there for authority? It would be reasonable to presume life would be charmed would it not? I hesitate to be so transparent to admit it took me a really long time to understand the depth of error in that question. God does not promise you an easy life; in fact, just the opposite.

John 16:33
*"I have told you these things, so that in me you may have peace. **In this world you will have trouble.** But take heart! I have overcome the world."*

Although you are in fellowship with the Lord laughing, talking, exchanging ideas, and seeing things from an entirely new perspective, there is a real enemy in this world determined to see you fail.

1 Peter 5:8
Be alert and of sober mind. Your enemy the devil prowls around like a roaring lion looking for someone to devour.

Ephesians 6:12
For our struggle is not against flesh and blood, but against the rulers, against the authorities, against the powers of this dark world and against the spiritual forces of evil in the heavenly realms.

As Jesus says in John 16:33 but take heart; I have overcome the world! Jesus died on the cross and rose again to defeat death; he defeated Satan. The battle has been won. If Satan has been defeated and the battle has been won, why do we have troubles in this world? Why do we experience so much pain? There are a lot of questions we will not be able to answer this side of heaven.

Isaiah 55:8
"My thoughts are nothing like your thoughts," says the Lord. "And my ways are far beyond anything you could imagine."

A study of scripture can enlighten you on the whys of Satan's dominion on earth until the return of our Lord, Jesus Christ. In the meantime, it can be comforting to know the enemy can only hurt you through the mind. You've probably heard some say,

"The battle is in the mind." Are you asking why on earth would that be comforting? When you are walking with the Lord and studying His ways and understand His favor, power, and authority you do not have to let the enemy have his way with your mind. You now have the authority to stand on Jesus. Yes, you have the right and authority to stand on the word of God. The word was made flesh – Jesus. Jesus is your rock, your foundation (the cornerstone); you can stand on God's word – Jesus. Proclaim His word. Stand.

2 Timothy 1:7
For God did not give us a spirit of fear. He gave us a spirit of power and of love and of a good mind.

There are times in my life my thoughts do not line up with God's truth and are anything but peaceful. Different times I've had to stand on His word and pray, "I cast down imaginations and bring my thoughts captive to the mind of Christ." Or the same thing said, "I reject that thought; it doesn't line up with the word of God as truth." I could list many other versions of my prayer but you get the gist. Stand. Pray a prayer based on scripture and stand on that truth to see you through. The word of God was made flesh; so when we stand based on scripture we stand with Jesus. Remember, he said, "Take heart; I've overcome the world!"

2 Corinthians 10:5
We are *destroying speculations and every lofty thing raised up against the knowledge of God, and* we are *taking every thought captive to the obedience of Christ,*

Jesus has authority over all things living and not living. Every knee shall bow to the name of Jesus.

Daniel 7:14
He was given authority, glory and sovereign power; all nations and peoples of every language worshiped him. His dominion is an everlasting dominion that will not pass away, and his kingdom is one that will never be destroyed.

Romans 14:11
It is written: "'As surely as I live,' says the Lord, 'every knee will bow before me; every tongue will acknowledge God.'"

When our focus is on Jesus and His fellowship, our thoughts line up with His thoughts and we glean from His favor, power, and authority. He is our friend with the benefits of peace in the midst of chaos, joy in the midst of pain, and the ability replace a negative thought or perspective with a His thought and perspective. In the friendships we are more familiar with; we can share our joys and pains and ask for advice and then have the choice to listen or not. We have the same choice with the Lord.

When we interact with him we choose to accept His truth or reject His truth. Different from other relationships, with the Lord we can know one hundred percent when He speaks it is absolutely the right answer. In my personal journey with the Lord, I am often slow to remember that awesome benefit!

Challenge:

As we wrap up our time together, I challenge you to go deeper. Continue to recognize God's presence in your present through awareness; engage Him; choose daily friendship with the Lord. Remember friendships at their best are two-way; He wants to share His desires as much as you want to share yours – let Him. Ask Him questions. Find out what is on His mind. Continue your journey. Stop. Look. Listen. Speak. Feel God's tangible presence. Watch for Him and invite Him into your daily details. Pray His word – praying is simply having a conversation; He loves to be reminded of what He said through His Word. Enjoy each other. He loves what you love and wants you to have joy. Find out more about the Joy of the Lord and how to experience it. Remember the best times with your friends are typically found in the most simplistic moments. In those easy moments we feel loved. Friendship with the Lord is all about loving and being loved in its most simplistic way.

Experience Him:

- Based on the scripture we can take our thoughts captive to the mind of Christ, write your own words to say when you need to shut the voice of the enemy up or any negative thought that drives you crazy. It doesn't have to be wordy; it simply has to be your words.
- Ask God to change your perspective to His perspective and to replace your thoughts with His thoughts.
- Do a word search and learn more about different characteristics and attributes of the Lord like joy, peace, love, power, and authority.
- Continue to practice, engage, notice, and grow in your friendship with the Lord; fall in love with Jesus.
- Say yes to God; stop what you are doing and simply say, "Yes, Lord."

Let's Pray:

Thank you Lord for this journey of friendship and getting to know you more and more. Thank you that you never leave us and as we seek more and more of you we will find you. Lord, you long to be in our details; continue to call out to us and let us be sensitive to hear your call. Show us the way, Lord, draw us close. We shout out in a loud voice of praise, YES, to your invitation.

In Your Son's Name – Jesus we pray.

Amen!

Conclusion

I have enjoyed putting together our journey this last month. I have laughed and cried; I have discovered so much more about myself. My personal friendship with the Lord has taken on entirely new and surprising directions. It has been fun, mostly. LOL (Laugh Out Loud) I would love to share with you some of my personal journey through this experience with you. I would love to hear some of your story. If you are interested in suggested resources to 'go deeper', please visit www.michellegreenministries.com for a guide to accompany each topic mentioned in each chapter. If you would like to read more about my experience and also share yours, please come and visit the blog site at www.MichelleGreenMinistries.com. The resource guide is a work in progress; the blog is just beginning, so visit me again and again and we will learn, experience, share, and grow together.

I cannot wait to meet you in cyberspace and hear about the wonderful time you are having with the Lord. Down the road I plan to have other options to meet you through interactive webinar options and conference calls.

Michelle Green

About The Author

Michelle Green is the author of "I Know You!" An Invitation from God "Let's Be Friends".

Michelle is also a Christian speaker and life coach and founder and CEO of Michelle Green Ministries

(www.MichelleGreenMinistries.com), a ministry dedicated to inspiring, equipping and activating intimacy with Father God.

She and her husband also are directors of non-profit organization: 72 Hours, Inc. (www.72hours42420.com)

They reside in Kentucky and enjoy family with their two sons, daughter-in-law, & two grandchildren.

www.ingramcontent.com/pod-product-compliance
Lightning Source LLC
Chambersburg PA
CBHW071025040426
42443CB00007B/932